contents

CW00672477

Letter from the Publisher

Dear Busy Reader,

Life is too short to be reading 300 page computer manuals! These days most people need to know how to perform a wide range of complicated computing tasks just so they can get their real job done. That's what gave me the idea for Go Guides. I wanted a series of simple guides to using my computer that could sit on my desk for instant access. I couldn't find such guides so I developed them myself.

These books cover a wide range of computer topics, from using your basic software programs to getting the most out of the Internet. They provide the information you need in a clear and concise format without getting you bogged down in computer jargon.

If there is any way you think these books can be improved please don't hesitate to email me at matthew@blake.com.au and to check out our latest releases go to our website at www.pascalpress.com.au.

Yours sincerely

Matthew Blake
Publisher

Copyright © Pascal Press 2001

ISBN 1 74020 262 7

Pascal Press
PO Box 250
Glebe NSW 2037
(02) 8585 4044
www.pascalpress.com.au

Text by Glenn Brown
Designed and typeset by Egan-Reid Ltd, Auckland
Printed in Singapore by Green Giant Press

the outlook window

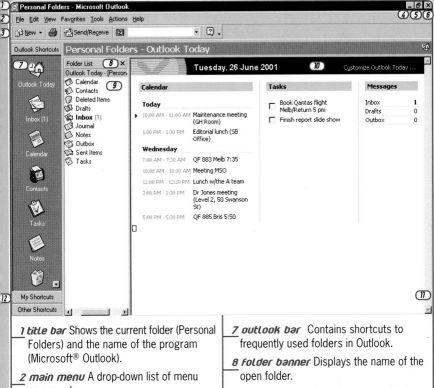

1 *title bar* Shows the current folder (Personal Folders) and the name of the program (Microsoft® Outlook).

2 *main menu* A drop-down list of menu commands.

3 *standard toolbar* Includes buttons for the common operations including creating a new mail message or other item, printing, Send/Receive, Address Book, Find and Help.

4 *minimise window* Reduces window to an icon on the taskbar.

5 *restore window* Returns window to previous size.

6 *close window* Shuts down Outlook.

7 *outlook bar* Contains shortcuts to frequently used folders in Outlook.

8 *folder banner* Displays the name of the open folder.

9 *folder list* Displays the personal folders available in your mailbox.

10 *outlook today* Shows a summary of the day's activities and tasks.

11 *vertical scroll bar* Used to move up and down through longer lists in the Outlook Today field.

12 *shortcuts* Areas for storing shortcuts to your commonly used folders.

resizing pages The various panes in the Outlook window can be resized easily. Simply move your mouse pointer over the border of a pane (such as the border between the Outlook Bar and the folder list) so that the mouse pointer turns into a double-headed arrow. Click and drag the border to change the size of the pane.

Note that the File menu will offer you different options depending on which part of Outlook you are viewing.

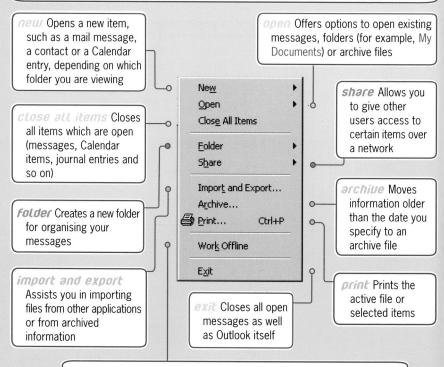

new Opens a new item, such as a mail message, a contact or a Calendar entry, depending on which folder you are viewing

open Offers options to open existing messages, folders (for example, My Documents) or archive files

close all items Closes all items which are open (messages, Calendar items, journal entries and so on)

share Allows you to give other users access to certain items over a network

folder Creates a new folder for organising your messages

archive Moves information older than the date you specify to an archive file

import and export Assists you in importing files from other applications or from archived information

exit Closes all open messages as well as Outlook itself

print Prints the active file or selected items

New
Open
Close All Items
Folder
Share
Import and Export...
Archive...
Print...   Ctrl+P
Work Offline
Exit

work offline Disconnects you from your Internet connection. Useful if you have received all your messages and don't want to waste your Internet connection hours while you read them

Other options on the File menu:
save as Saves the active item with a different file name, location or file format
save attachment Saves a file attached to an email to a location you specify
print preview Shows how a file will look on the page when you print it

saving email as text If you want to minimise the number of emails you have but want to keep the information, you can easily save a mail message as a text file and put it on a disk or your hard drive. Select the message in your Inbox, click on the File menu and choose Save As. In the Save as type box, choose Text Files (*.txt). Select a location from the folders to save the file, give it a name and click Save.

the edit menu

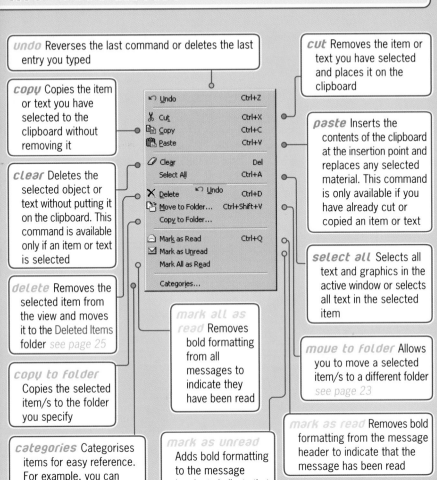

undo Reverses the last command or deletes the last entry you typed

copy Copies the item or text you have selected to the clipboard without removing it

clear Deletes the selected object or text without putting it on the clipboard. This command is available only if an item or text is selected

delete Removes the selected item from the view and moves it to the Deleted Items folder *see page 25*

copy to folder Copies the selected item/s to the folder you specify

categories Categorises items for easy reference. For example, you can assign categories such as Business, Personal and so on to your emails. You can also define your own categories to organise messages or appointments

mark all as read Removes bold formatting from all messages to indicate they have been read

mark as unread Adds bold formatting to the message header to indicate that the message has not been read. This is useful if you want to remind yourself to respond to a message at a later time

cut Removes the item or text you have selected and places it on the clipboard

paste Inserts the contents of the clipboard at the insertion point and replaces any selected material. This command is only available if you have already cut or copied an item or text

select all Selects all text and graphics in the active window or selects all text in the selected item

move to folder Allows you to move a selected item/s to a different folder *see page 23*

mark as read Removes bold formatting from the message header to indicate that the message has been read

Menu items shown:
- Undo — Ctrl+Z
- Cut — Ctrl+X
- Copy — Ctrl+C
- Paste — Ctrl+V
- Clear — Del
- Select All — Ctrl+A
- Delete — Ctrl+D
- Move to Folder... — Ctrl+Shift+V
- Copy to Folder...
- Mark as Read — Ctrl+Q
- Mark as Unread
- Mark All as Read
- Categories...

assigning categories to messages Outlook can help you assign categories automatically to your email based on the identity of the recipient or the contents of the message. This enables you to group, sort or filter the items and view each category separately if you wish. To assign a category to emails, click on the Tools menu and select Rules Wizard. Then choose New. Choose either the Assign categories to sent messages or the Assign categories based on content option and then follow the wizard as it guides you through the types of messages to which the rule should apply.

Note that the View menu will change depending on what part of Outlook you are viewing. The following View menu appears when you have your Inbox on your screen, but will have different options if, for example, you are viewing your Calendar or Task list.

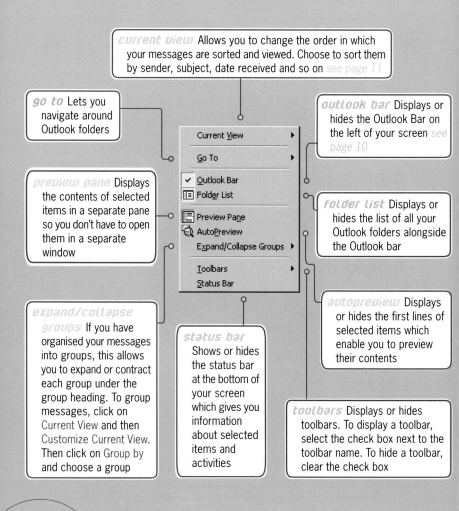

current view Allows you to change the order in which your messages are sorted and viewed. Choose to sort them by sender, subject, date received and so on see page 11

go to Lets you navigate around Outlook folders

outlook bar Displays or hides the Outlook Bar on the left of your screen see page 10

preview pane Displays the contents of selected items in a separate pane so you don't have to open them in a separate window

folder list Displays or hides the list of all your Outlook folders alongside the Outlook bar

Current View
Go To
✓ Outlook Bar
Folder List
Preview Pane
AutoPreview
Expand/Collapse Groups
Toolbars
Status Bar

expand/collapse groups If you have organised your messages into groups, this allows you to expand or contract each group under the group heading. To group messages, click on Current View and then Customize Current View. Then click on Group by and choose a group

status bar Shows or hides the status bar at the bottom of your screen which gives you information about selected items and activities

autopreview Displays or hides the first lines of selected items which enable you to preview their contents

toolbars Displays or hides toolbars. To display a toolbar, select the check box next to the toolbar name. To hide a toolbar, clear the check box

checking spelling Outlook can be set to automatically check your spelling before sending a message. To do this, simply click on the Tools menu, choose Options and click on the Spelling tab. Click in the box marked Always check spelling before sending. If you want to turn this option off, simply follow the same steps and clear the checkbox.

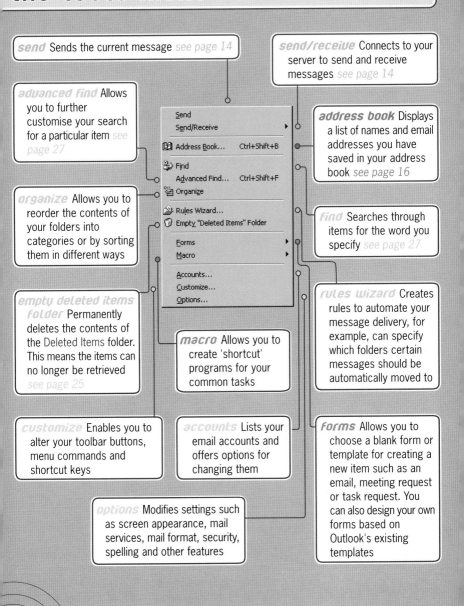

send Sends the current message see page 14

send/receive Connects to your server to send and receive messages see page 14

advanced find Allows you to further customise your search for a particular item see page 27

address book Displays a list of names and email addresses you have saved in your address book see page 16

organize Allows you to reorder the contents of your folders into categories or by sorting them in different ways

find Searches through items for the word you specify see page 27

empty deleted items folder Permanently deletes the contents of the Deleted Items folder. This means the items can no longer be retrieved see page 25

rules wizard Creates rules to automate your message delivery, for example, can specify which folders certain messages should be automatically moved to

macro Allows you to create 'shortcut' programs for your common tasks

customize Enables you to alter your toolbar buttons, menu commands and shortcut keys

accounts Lists your email accounts and offers options for changing them

forms Allows you to choose a blank form or template for creating a new item such as an email, meeting request or task request. You can also design your own forms based on Outlook's existing templates

options Modifies settings such as screen appearance, mail services, mail format, security, spelling and other features

Menu items shown:
Send
Send/Receive
Address Book... Ctrl+Shift+B
Find
Advanced Find... Ctrl+Shift+F
Organize
Rules Wizard...
Empty "Deleted Items" Folder
Forms
Macro
Accounts...
Customize...
Options...

changing features Outlook automatically customises menus and toolbars for you based on how often you use the commands. When you first start Outlook, only the most basic commands appear. Then, as you work, Outlook adjusts the menus and toolbars so that only the commands and toolbar buttons you use most often appear on your screen.

Note that the Actions menu will change depending on what part of Outlook you are viewing. The following Actions menu appears when you have your Inbox on your screen, but will have different options if, for example, you are viewing your Calendar or task list.

new mail message Creates a new blank email message see page 14

new fax Opens a new fax form

flag for follow up Attaches a small flag icon to an item to remind you to follow it up

more stationery Displays a list of additional stationery to spice up your emails. The designs can only be viewed by recipients whose email programs can read HTML messages

find all Search for items by keywords of your choosing

Menu items:
- New Mail Message   Ctrl+N
- New Fax Message
- New Mail Message Using ▶
  - More Stationery...
  - Microsoft Word (Plain Text)
  - Microsoft Office ▶
  - Plain Text
  - Microsoft Outlook Rich Text
  - HTML (No Stationery)
- Flag for Follow Up...   Ctrl+Shift+G
- Find All ▶
- Junk E-mail ▶
- Reply   Ctrl+R
- Reply to All   Ctrl+Shift+R
- Forward   Ctrl+F

microsoft word (plain text) Opens a new message using Microsoft® Word as your email editor

junk e-mail Enables you to specify certain senders as junk or adult content email senders and automatically move messages from these senders out of your Inbox see page 15

plain text Opens a new message using plain text (without any formatting or pictures)

microsoft office Opens a new message using either a Word document, a PowerPoint slide, an Excel worksheet or Access data page

reply Opens up a new message window automatically addressed to the sender of the email highlighted in your Inbox

reply to all If the email you have highlighted in your Inbox was addressed to more than one person, this will open up a new message window addressed to all of those recipients. Use this wisely!

microsoft outlook rich text Opens a new message using rich text (which allows formatting)

forward Automatically puts a copy of a message into a new message so you can send it on to someone else

HTML (no stationery) Opens a new blank message with no design stationery on it but which allows formatting

tip

message formats Microsoft® Outlook can read email in a range of different formats including pictures, stationery and other objects. Emails which use stationery are formatted as HTML, that is, special encoded text which is most commonly used on the Internet to create web pages. Be aware, however, that not all people have an email program which can read HTML emails. Plain text email, on the other hand, can be read by all email programs.

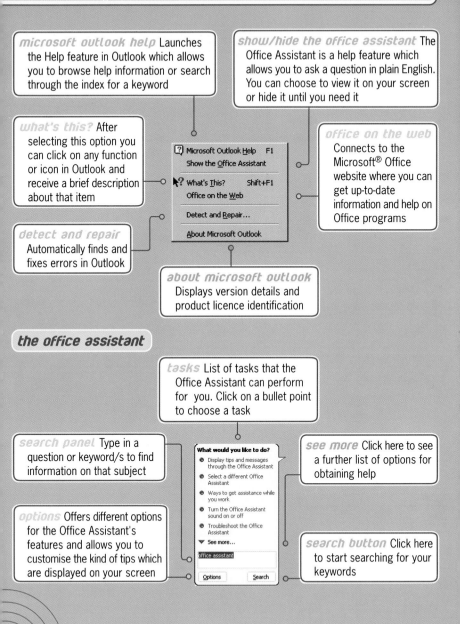

microsoft outlook help Launches the Help feature in Outlook which allows you to browse help information or search through the index for a keyword

show/hide the office assistant The Office Assistant is a help feature which allows you to ask a question in plain English. You can choose to view it on your screen or hide it until you need it

what's this? After selecting this option you can click on any function or icon in Outlook and receive a brief description about that item

office on the web Connects to the Microsoft® Office website where you can get up-to-date information and help on Office programs

detect and repair Automatically finds and fixes errors in Outlook

about microsoft outlook Displays version details and product licence identification

Microsoft Outlook Help   F1
Show the Office Assistant
What's This?   Shift+F1
Office on the Web
Detect and Repair...
About Microsoft Outlook

the office assistant

tasks List of tasks that the Office Assistant can perform for you. Click on a bullet point to choose a task

search panel Type in a question or keyword/s to find information on that subject

see more Click here to see a further list of options for obtaining help

options Offers different options for the Office Assistant's features and allows you to customise the kind of tips which are displayed on your screen

search button Click here to start searching for your keywords

What would you like to do?
• Display tips and messages through the Office Assistant
• Select a different Office Assistant
• Ways to get assistance while you work
• Turn the Office Assistant sound on or off
• Troubleshoot the Office Assistant
▼ See more...
office assistant
Options   Search

getting help Use the Office Assistant to find out answers to your questions. If you can't see it on your screen, click Show the Office Assistant on the Help menu and then type a question into the Office Assistant's search panel. Then click on the Search button.

The Outlook Bar contains shortcuts to frequently used Outlook folders as well as your local network, your computer's hard drive and the Internet. You can also create your own shortcuts to put on the Outlook Bar.

outlook today View Calendar, tasks and email folders on a single screen see page 3

calendar See schedules and details of appointments in day, week and month views. You can set reminders for your appointments and specify how others view your Calendar by designating the time an appointment takes see pages 18 and 21

contacts A contact is a person or organisation you correspond with. You can store information about contacts such as email addresses, job titles, phone numbers, addresses and notes see pages 16–17

my shortcuts A place to make your own shortcuts to your frequently used Outlook folders

Outlook Shortcuts

Outlook Today

Inbox (1)

Calendar

Contacts

Tasks

Notes

My Shortcuts

Other Shortcuts

tasks A task is a personal or work-related errand you want to track through to completion. Outlook displays your tasks in a table. Overdue tasks appear in red see page 19

notes Use notes to jot down questions, ideas, reminders and anything you would write on notepaper. Notes are also useful for storing bits of information you may need later, such as directions or text you want to reuse in other items or documents see page 22

other shortcuts Create links to My Document, My Computer and Internet Favorites folders see page 26

deleted items Stores deleted items where they can be recovered or permanently deleted see page 25

adding groups and shortcuts to the outlook bar To add a group to the Outlook Bar, right click the background of the bar and click Add New Group on the shortcut menu. Type a name for the group and then press Enter. To add shortcuts to a group, simply right click the group and choose Outlook Bar Shortcut. Then choose the folder you would like to create a shortcut to.

the current view submenu 11

The Current View submenu allows you to sort your messages, journal entries or tasks into different orders. To access this submenu, **click** on the View menu and **move** your mouse pointer down to Current View.

messages Shows messages in Inbox

messages with autopreview View the first three lines of an email message without opening the message

by follow up flag View messages which have been marked with a flag for you to follow up (use the Actions menu to flag items for follow up)

last seven days View messages from the last seven days only

flagged for next seven days View messages that have been flagged for follow-up action that are due in the next seven days

by conversation topic View messages grouped according to their subject headers. For example, if a number of people have sent you email with the same subject line, this feature will group them all together

by sender View messages from individual senders

format columns Allows you to change the style of the columns you see

unread messages View messages that are marked as unread

sent to View messages according to who they were sent to. This is useful if you want to separate out the messages sent to you personally and those sent to other people or groups of people

define views Enables you to change the style and contents of each of the available views. For example, you can specify which column headings you will see when you view your emails or journal entries

message timeline View messages represented by icons in the order that they were sent to you

customize current view Gives you a summary of all the features available in your current view

Menu items: Messages, Messages with AutoPreview, By Follow-up Flag, Last Seven Days, Flagged for Next Seven Days, By Conversation Topic, By Sender, Unread Messages, Sent To, Message Timeline, Customize Current View..., Define Views..., Format Columns...

tip changing the view To change the way you view a folder, you can either switch from the active view to another standard view (for example, by choosing List, Small Icons or Large Icons from the View menu), or you can keep your current view settings but reorganise the information. Using the View menu you can group, sort or filter your items. You can also add or remove columns or fields, and change fonts and other formatting to your liking.

The Contacts database in Outlook allows you to build up details of people or companies with whom you regularly communicate. You can choose how much detail to include for each contact. To access the New Contact dialog box, **click** on the File menu, **move** your mouse pointer to New and **click** Contact (or use the keyboard shortcut Ctrl + Shift + C).

general Fill in general fields as shown here, including email and street addresses and phone numbers. Also allows you to specify the format you send your contacts email in (plain text or more complex HTML format)

activities Tracks tasks, appointments, email, notes or documents related to a contact. Items or documents can also be linked to a contact using this feature

certificates Sets the security features that allow you to send and receive secure email messages and prevent unauthorised access to your computer

all fields Allows you to define your own headings for information about your contacts that may not be included elsewhere

details Includes more detailed information about a contact's professional and personal status such as department, birthday and assistant's or manager's name

notes area Make general notes about each contact

categories Choose a category for this contact, such as Business or Personal

private Allows you to hide a contact from any other users who have access to your contact list

different addresses Outlook gives you space to include more than one address for each of your contacts. You can include a business and a home address and up to three email addresses. You can then specify which email address is the one used when you send each contact a message. Click on the down arrow next to E-mail to add additional addresses.

For more information on Contacts, see page 17

A shortcut is a fast and simple way of completing a task using the keyboard rather than using the mouse. For example, a quick way to create a new mail message in Outlook is to hold down the Ctrl key and press N. [Ctrl + N] is an example of a keyboard shortcut. Shortcuts will make you a much faster user of Microsoft® Outlook. (Note: not all keyboards have a Windows key as used in the Windows shortcuts below.)

Inbox shortcuts

Open the Address Book	[Ctrl + Shift + B]
Open the Inbox	[Ctrl + Shift + I]
Open the Outbox	[Ctrl + Shift + O]
Create a new mail message	[Ctrl + Shift + M]
Reply to the sender of the currently selected message	[Ctrl + R]
Reply to all recipients of the currently selected message	[Ctrl + Shift + R]
Check for new mail	[Ctrl + M]
Mark selected message as read	[Ctrl + Q]
Forward the selected message	[Ctrl + F]

calendar

Create a new appointment	[Ctrl + Shift + A]
Create a new meeting request	[Ctrl + Shift + Q]

tasks

Create a new task	[Ctrl + Shift + K]
Create a new task request	[Ctrl + Shift + U]

windows shortcuts

AutoRun	[⊞ + R]
Find files	[⊞ + F]
Minimise screen	[⊞ + M]
Open Windows Explorer	[⊞ + E]

notes

Create a new note	[Ctrl + Shift + N]

general

Create a new folder	[Ctrl + Shift + E]
Print selected item	[Ctrl + P]
Delete selected item/s and move to Deleted Items folder	[Ctrl + D]
Move selected item to another folder	[Ctrl + Shift + V]
Jump back to beginning of an item	[Ctrl + Home]
Jump to the end of an item	[Ctrl + End]
Jump one screen length forwards	[Ctrl + Page Down]
Jump one screen length back	[Ctrl + Page Up]
Help	[F1]
Search for items	[F3]

editing shortcuts

Bold text	[Ctrl + B]
Italic text	[Ctrl + I]
Underline text	[Ctrl + U]
Cut selection	[Ctrl + X]
Copy selection	[Ctrl + C]
Paste copied or cut selection	[Ctrl + V]
Select all	[Ctrl + A]
Add bulleted list	[Ctrl + Shift + L]
Clear all formatting	[Ctrl + spacebar]

14   sending and receiving mail

Before you start, make sure your Outlook Bar is visible. If not, **click** on the View menu and **select** Outlook Bar. Also make sure the Standard toolbar is visible by **clicking** on the View menu, **selecting** Toolbars and ensuring that Standard is ticked.

Receiving new mail

To check for new messages, simply **click** on the Send/Receive button on the Standard toolbar.

📑 Send/Receive
The Send/ Receive button

Composing a new message

1 **Click** on the File menu.
2 **Move** your mouse pointer to New and **click** on Mail Message.
3 In the To... panel, **type** the email address of the person to whom you are sending the message. To send the message to more than one recipient, **add** a comma or a semicolon and a space between each address in the To... box
4 In the Cc... box, **type** the addresses of anyone to whom you would like to send a courtesy copy of the message.
5 In the Subject panel, **type** a brief description of your message.
6 **Type** your message in the main window.
7 **Click** the Send button on the toolbar. Your message will move to the Outbox and then to Sent Items when it has been sent.

Addressing a new message

The Send button

Checking your spelling in a message

Before you send your message, **click** on the Tools menu and **select** Spelling. The spelling check will begin scanning your message and will stop at each word it doesn't recognise. You can choose an alternate spelling from those offered (**select** a word from the list and **click** Change), ignore the suggestion (**click** Ignore), or add the word to your custom dictionary (**click** Add).

Spelling check [F7]

Attaching a file to an email

When you have typed your message:
1 **Click** on the Insert menu and select File.
2 **Browse** your folders until you find the file you want and **click** on the file.
3 **Click** on Insert and choose Insert as Attachment.

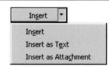
Choose Insert as Attachment

tip

sending messages If you want to save your email but not send it immediately, click on the File menu and choose Save. This will move your message to the Drafts folder. You can then view and edit the message by opening the Drafts folder and double-clicking the message. When you're ready to send the message, click the Send button as usual.

Organising the contents of folders

To organise the contents of your folders:

1 **Click** on the Organize button on the toolbar.

The Organize button on the toolbar

This feature allows you to move messages in and out of different folders, or move them to your calendar or other areas of Outlook. There are many ways to organise your items: experiment with the options offered here.

Organising a folder

Managing junk email

If you find you receive unsolicited advertising or other messages, Outlook can search for certain keywords and automatically move messages containing these phrases from your Inbox to another folder (such as Deleted Items) before you even see them. To move jumk email to your Deleted Items folder:

1 **Click** on the Actions menu and **choose** Junk E-mail.
2 In the bulleted items for Junk messages, in each of the first lists, **click** Move. The second list on each line will change from a list of colors to a list of folder destinations.
3 **Click** Deleted Items.
4 **Click** Turn On.

When you first use this feature, it is a good idea to check which messages are being moved to your Deleted Items folder before you empty this folder in case any legitimate messages are being removed.

Archiving old messages

Saving old messages out to a separate archive file will reduce the space taken up by your Inbox. To manually transfer old items to a storage file:

1 **Click** on the File menu and **choose** Archive.
2 **Choose** from the options offered.

Setting AutoArchive options

You can have also have old items automatically transferred to your archive folder using the AutoArchive feature. Items are considered old when they reach the age you specify. **Click** on the Tools menu, **choose** Options, **click** on the Other tab and **click** on AutoArchive to view the options.

good housekeeping It can be easy to let your Inbox get overloaded with old messages which take up valuable space on your hard drive or network server. Remember to periodically clear your Deleted Items folder and delete old emails from your Inbox that you no longer need. Also archive your old messages, as described above, when possible.

Outlook stores basic details about your Contacts in your Personal Address Book. You can also use the Contacts feature to keep a more detailed record of your interactions.

Adding an email address to Contacts and Personal Address Book

1 **Open** a message sent to you by the person whose name you'd like to add.
2 In the From... panel, **right click** your mouse over the name or email address of the sender.
3 **Select** Add to Contacts from the shortcut menu. This will add the sender to your Contacts list and your Address Book.

Adding a sender to your Contacts and Address Book

To add details to your Personal Address Book from scratch:
1 **Click** on the Tools menu and select Address Book.
2 **Click** the New button on the toolbar and **click** on New Contact.

Adding an email using the Personal Address Book

To address an email using your Personal Address Book:
1 Open a new message (Ctrl + Shift + M) and **click** the To... button.
2 In the Show Names From drop-down list, **select** Contacts.
3 **Select** the person's name from the list on the left and **click** To... to move it into the list of recipients for the email.
4 **Repeat** the process to select additional recipients, **selecting** (if you prefer) Cc... to send a courtesy copy of the message or Bcc... to send a 'blind' copy (the names of the 'blind' recipients cannot be seen by any other recipients).
5 **Click** OK to return to your message.

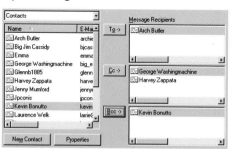

Selecting recipients from the Address Book

using Word to create your emails You can specify Microsoft® Word as your default email editor, and then use it to create all your messages. To do this, click on the Tools menu, select Options and then click on the Mail Format tab at the top of the dialog box. Tick the checkbox next to Use Microsoft Word to edit email messages. Then click OK.

Adding a new Contact

To add a new Contact to your Contacts database from scratch:

1 **Click** on the File menu and **move** your mouse pointer to New.
2 **Click** Contact. (Alternatively, you can use the keyboard shortcut Ctrl + Shift + C.) This will open the New Contact dialog box as shown on page 12.
3 **Type** in the details for the Contact. Don't forget to **click** on the different tabs along the top of the dialog box for futher options.
4 **Click** OK when you have finished.

Viewing your Contacts

1 On the Outlook Bar, **click** on Contacts.
2 **Double-click** on the name of the contact you want to see. This brings up the contact details window for this person whose details can be edited from this point.

The Contact can be emailed from here by clicking on the New Message button on the toolbar.

Viewing your Contacts

Updating your Contacts

1 **Open** the Contact as described above.
2 On the General and Details tabs, update the information you want.
3 **Click** OK.

Importing and exporting Contacts

The Import and Export Wizard on the File menu allows you to import email addresses and contact information from other applications or from archived information you have previously stored.

The Import and Export Wizard

Importing information from a file or personal folder file

1 **Click** on the File menu and choose Import and Export.
2 **Click** Import from another program or file.
3 Follow the instructions in the Import and Export Wizard which follows.

Exporting items to a file or to a personal folder file

1 **Click** on the File menu and **choose** Import and Export.
2 **Click** Export to a file.
3 Follow the instructions in the Import and Export Wizard which follows.

user-defined fields Each Contact dialog box has an All Fields tab. Use this feature to define different kinds of information for each contact.

Adding an appointment to your Calendar

1 **Click** on Calendar on the Outlook Bar.
2 Using the monthly calendar on the right hand side of your screen, **click** on the day you would like to add an appointment to.
3 **Double-click** on the time your appointment starts using the blank daily calendar on the left of the screen.

Adding an appointment

4 **Type** in a subject and a location.
5 **Specify** the end time for the appointment and any other features which are appropriate.
6 **Click** Save and Close on the toolbar.

Scheduling recurring appointments

To change an Outlook appointment from a one-time event to a recurring appointment:

1 **Open** the appointment by double-clicking on it in your Calendar.
2 **Click** on Recurrence on the toolbar.
3 **Click** on Daily, Weekly, Monthly or Yearly, depending on how often the meeting will recur. You can also schedule meetings to recur a certain number of weeks apart by **typing** in the number of weeks for the recurrence in the relevant panel.

Setting the recurrence of an appointment

4 **Select** a Start and End date for the appointment if appropriate.
5 **Click** OK.

Scheduling holidays

The Calendar allows you to automatically add the national holidays for any country into your Calendar. To do this:

1 **Click** on the Tools menu and select Options.
2 **Click** on the Preferences tab.
3 **Click** Calendar Options and **click** Add Holidays.
4 **Select** the countries whose holidays you would like to see on your Calendar.
5 **Click** OK.

Adding holidays

viewing your calendar There are numerous ways to view your Outlook Calendar. You can choose a one-day, a five-day (work week), a seven-day, or a full-month view using the icons on the toolbar. If your toolbar is not visible, click on the View menu ⇒Toolbars ⇒ Standard to display it. To see other ways to view your Calendar, open your Calendar, choose View menu ⇒ Current View and select an option from the list.

A task is a personal or work-related errand you want to track through to its completion. A recurring task can repeat at regular intervals or repeat based on the date you mark the task complete. For example, you might want to send a status report to your manager on the last Friday of every month, or get a haircut when one month has passed since your last one.

Creating a new task

1 On the Outlook Bar, **click** Tasks.
2 **Click** in the panel which says Click here to add a new Task.
3 **Type** in details of your task.
4 **Type** in a due date for the task and **press** Enter.

**Adding a new task
to the task list**

Opening and editing a task

1 On the Outlook Bar, **click** Tasks.
2 Find the task in the task list and **double-click** on it.

Now you can set various options for your task:

- Make the task recurring by **clicking** on Recurrence on the toolbar and setting options.

Editing a task

- **Type** notes about your task in the blank notes section at the bottom.
- **Click** on the Details tab to keep track of the time and other resources you have spent on a task.

Assigning a task

You can send a task request to another person if you would like them to complete the task:

Assign Task

The Assign Task button

1 **Open** your task for editing as described above.
2 On the toolbar, **click** on Assign Task.
3 In the To... panel, type in the email address of the person you want to send the task to (or **click** on the To... button to select a Contact).
4 **Set** the options you require and **click** the Send button on the toolbar.

When you send a task request, the recipient can accept, decline or reassign the task. If it is accepted, you will no longer be able to change important details of the task such as its due date. The recipient becomes the 'owner' of the task and is the only person who can make those changes. However you will still be able to see the task's progress through your own task list.

setting reminders You can have Outlook remind you of a task at a certain time on a particular day. Open the task as described above and click the Reminder checkbox. Use the drop-down menus to specify a date and a time for the reminder. At this time a dialog box will pop up on your screen to remind you of the task.

20   USING the Journal

The Outlook Journal is a way of recording your activities relating to certain Contacts and also of tracking every Office document you edit in your day-to-day activities. Entries in the Journal are organised by the last time you modified them, but you can organise them in many different ways.

Opening a Journal entry

1 On the Outlook Bar or in your folder list, **click** Journal.
2 **Right click** the journal entry and **click** Open Journal Entry or Open Item Referred To on the shortcut menu.

Journal entries

Specifying Journal options

The Journal can record your interactions (for example, emails, meetings and tasks) with each of your contacts. To specify what activities to view for each contact:
1 **Click** the Tools menu and **choose** Options.
2 **Click** the Preferences tab.
3 **Click** Journal Options.
4 Select what Journal entries you would like to view and which contacts you would like them to apply to.
5 **Click** OK and then OK again.

Choosing what Journal entries to view

Options for opening Journal entries

Outlook allows you to specify what happens when you double-click on a Journal entry. You can choose to simply open the entry or open the actual document that is referred to. To do this:
1 **Click** the Tools menu and **choose** Options.
2 **Click** the Preferences tab.
3 **Click** Journal Options.
4 **Click** Opens the journal entry or Opens the item referred to by the journal entry depending on what you prefer.

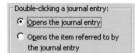

Choosing to open Journal entries or items

viewing journal entries for a contact To view all the Journal entries relating to a particular contact, first open the contact you wish to view and then click the Activities tab. In the Show box, click Journal. A list will appear of all your interactions with that contact.

Outlook allows you to plan meetings using your Calendar. If you work in an organisation in which everyone uses Outlook, you can choose a meeting time which fits in with everyone's schedules and send a meeting request via email which alerts attendees to the meeting details.

Getting started
1 On the Outlook Bar, **click** Calendar.
2 **Click** on the Actions menu and select Plan a Meeting.

Inviting other people
1 **Click** on Invite Others. Your Contacts list will now be visible.
2 **Click** on the first attendee in your Contact list and **click** on Required or Optional.
3 **Repeat** this step for each attendee.
4 If you have meeting rooms or other resources (for example, audio visual equipment) listed in your Contacts list and you are required to book them, select the room or resource you would like to use and **click** Resources.
5 **Click** OK.

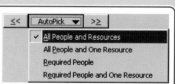

Selecting Contacts to invite to a meeting

Choosing a time
You will now see a list of your attendees and their schedules. The times in which your attendees are busy will be marked in blue on the Calendar.
1 Using the drop-down lists at the bottom of the dialog box, **nominate** a start time and an end time for your meeting. Outlook will alert you of any timing clashes.
2 If your attendees have a lot of time taken up already, you can use the AutoPick function to select the first available time. **Click** on AutoPick and select All People and Resources.
3 If you still can't find a suitable meeting time, click on AutoPick again and select Required People and One Resource. This will remove any Optional attendees from consideration.

Using AutoPick to select a time

Sending the meeting request
1 When you have a suitable time, **click** Make Meeting. This will bring up a meeting request dialog box.
2 **Type** in a subject and a location for your meeting.
3 **Check** that the meeting time is correct.
4 **Type** in a message to attendees in the bottom panel.
5 **Click** on the Send button on the toolbar.

The meeting request

sending agendas or minutes You can easily attach a file to your meeting request if you want to include agendas or previous minutes. Before you send the request, click on the Insert menu and choose File, then select the file to attach. Click on Open and choose Insert as Attachment from the drop-down menu. Then click Send.

About Notes
Notes are the electronic equivalent of paper sticky notes. You can use them to jot down questions, ideas, reminders or anything you would usually write on notepaper. Notes are also useful for storing bits of information you may need later, such as directions or text you want to re-use in other items or documents. You can leave notes open on the screen while you work. When you change a note, the changes are saved automatically.

Creating a Note
1 **Click** on the File menu, move the mouse pointer to New and **click** Note.
2 **Type** the text of the note.
3 To close the note, **click** the icon in the upper left corner of the Note window and then **click** Close.

Creating a new Note

Creating a folder for Notes
You can create a subfolder to store your notes in:
1 **Click** on the folder you would like your new folder to be included in. (You can do this on the Outlook Bar or in your folder list.)
2 **Right click** the mouse and **select** New Folder.
3 **Type** in a name for your folder.
4 In the Folder contains panel, **click** on the drop-down menu and **select** Note Items.
5 **Click** OK.

**Creating a folder
for Note items**

Copying text to a Note
You can copy text from any Outlook items (emails, Contacts, Calendar and so on) to a Note:
1 **Select** the text or item you would like to copy.
2 **Click and drag** the selected text over to the Notes icon on the Outlook Bar (or onto the Notes folder in the folder list).
3 **Release** the mouse button. A new note will be created with the selected text in it.

Sending a Note via email
1 **Click** on the Note icon in the upper left corner of your Note.
2 **Click** on Forward.
3 **Address** and **send** the email as usual. Your Note will be included as an attachment.

**Forwarding a Note
via email**

saving notes If you have a particularly lengthy note, you can save it as a separate file. Click on the Note icon in the top left corner of your Note and select Save As. From the Save as type drop-down menu, select the kind of file you want to save it as (plain text, Rich Text Format and so on) and browse through your folders for a location to save it to. Click Save.

Creating folders   23

Outlook allows you to create subfolders to organise your mail messages, notes and other items. Rather than having one long list of emails in your Inbox, for example, consider creating folders for different subject areas or senders. You can also create new folders on your computer's hard drive using Outlook.

Creating a new folder within Outlook

1 **Click** on the folder you would like your new folder to be included in. (You can do this on the Outlook Bar or in your folder list.)
2 **Right click** the mouse and **select** New Folder.
3 **Type** in a name for your folder.
4 In the Folder contains panel, **click** on the drop-down menu and **select** the type of items which will be included in your folder.
5 **Click** OK.

Creating a new folder for emails inside the Inbox

Moving an item to a folder

1 **Right click** the mouse over the item.
2 **Select** Move to Folder.
3 **Select** the folder to move it to and **click** OK.
Note: You can also click and drag items into folders in the folder list. (To view the folder list, **click** on the View menu and **select** Folder List.)

Moving an item to a folder

Creating a new folder in My Computer

1 On the Outlook Bar, **click** Other or Other Shortcuts.
2 **Click** My Computer.
3 **Double-click** the drive you want the new folder located on.
4 If you want to create the folder inside another folder, **double-click** that folder.
5 **Click** on the File menu, **move** the mouse pointer to New and then **click** Folder.
6 **Type** a name for the new folder.

My Computer on the Outlook Bar

folder management Large folders interfere with Outlook's performance, and you'll find that over time Outlook's folders grow if you don't regularly remove out-of-date messages. Check out a folder to see if it needs paring down by right-clicking it and selecting Properties. Then click the General tab and select the Folder Size button.

Viewing the Web toolbar

1 **Click** on the View menu.
2 **Move** your mouse pointer to Toolbars and **click** on Web.

Opening a web page

1 In the Address panel on the Web toolbar, **type** the
   address for the web page you would like to access.
2 Press Enter.

**The Address panel
on the Web toolbar**

Adding a web page to your Favorites

The Favorites menu allows you to save a shortcut to your favourite
web pages for easy access later.

1 **Open** the web page you would like to add.
2 **Click** on the Favorites menu and **select** Add to Favorites.
3 **Type** in a name for the web page (or leave the name as it is).
4 **Click** Add.

**Adding a web page to
the Favorites menu**

Opening a web page from Favorites

1 **Click** on the Favorites menu.
2 **Click** on the page you would like to visit.

Saving a calendar as a web page

You can save a calendar as a web page so that you can share
it with others. You can then specify the start and end dates,
include appointment details that are entered in the text section
of the appointment, and add a background colour or image. To
do this:

**Saving a calendar
as a web page**

1 **Click** on the View menu, **move** your mouse pointer to Go To
   and **click** Calendar.
2 **Click** on the File menu and **select** Save as Web Page. If you don't have the Internet Explorer
   Web Publishing Wizard installed, you will receive a prompt that tells you how to install it.
3 Under Duration, **type** a start date in the Start Date panel and **type** an end date in the End
   Date box.
4 Under Options, **choose** the options that you want.
5 **Type** a title for the calendar in the Calendar title box.
6 In the File Name panel, **type** the path to the location where you want to save the files and
   then **click** Save.

preventing viruses Malicious computer viruses, such as the infamous 'I
Love You' bug, work their infernal magic by exploiting security weaknesses
in communications software and mail programs. Most are delivered by a
seemingly innocent email which then infects your computer with the virus.
Don't be a victim: install a reputable anti-virus program (such as Norton
AntiVirus, Pc-cillin or McAfee) and keep it up to date.

Deleting mail messages

The Delete button

When you delete an Outlook item, it is moved to the Deleted Items folder in case you need to retrieve it.

1 **Select** the message you would like to delete from your Inbox or other folder. You can select more than one message by **holding down** the Ctrl key while you **click** on each message you want to delete.

2 **Click** the Delete button on the toolbar (or the Del key on your keyboard).

Deleting a task

1 In the task list, **select** the tasks you want to delete.

2 **Click** the Delete button on the toolbar (or the Del key on your keyboard).

Note: Deleting a task which you have assigned to someone else will only remove it from your task list. The task will remain in the task list of the person who accepted it, but you will no longer receive status reports for that task.

Retrieving a deleted item

1 On the Outlook Bar, **click** Outlook Shortcuts and then **click** Deleted Items.

2 **Select** the items you want to retrieve.

3 **Right click** the selection and then **click** Move to Folder on the menu.

4 In the Move the selected items to the folder panel, **click** the folder you want to move the items to.

The Deleted Items folder

Emptying the Deleted Items folder

You should try to empty your Deleted Items folder on a regular basis when you are sure you won't be needing the deleted items again. This will permanently remove the items from your system. To do this:

1 On the Outlook Bar, **click** Outlook Shortcuts.

2 **Right click** the mouse over the Deleted Items icon.

3 **Select** Empty "Deleted Items" folder from the submenu.

Emptying Deleted Items folder

quick retrieval To quickly retrieve a deleted item, click on the Deleted Items icon or folder, and click and drag the item from the Deleted Items folder to another folder of your choice.

You can access your saved documents and other files through Outlook without having to use Windows Explorer or return to the desktop at all.

Viewing the Advanced toolbar

If you use Outlook to access all your documents, it is a good idea to view the Advanced toolbar on your screen. This enables you to navigate through your folders more easily.

The Back and Forward buttons

1 **Click** on the View menu and **move** your mouse pointer to Toolbars.
2 **Click** on Advanced.

The Back and Forward arrow buttons allow you to jump back to the previous folder you opened and then move forward again.

The Up One Level button also allows you to jump up one level in your hierarchy of folders.

The Up One Level button

Opening a document from My Computer

1 On the Outlook Bar, **click** Other or Other Shortcuts.
2 **Click** My Computer.
3 **Browse** through the folders until you find the file you want to open. (Use the navigation buttons on the Advanced toolbar to help you.)
4 **Double-click** on the file to open it.
    Note: You can also jump directly to the My Documents folder by **clicking** on the My Documents icon on the Outlook Bar.

Opening My Computer or My Documents from the Outlook Bar

Changing the folder display

You can choose to display the contents of your folders in a number of ways. **Click** on the Current View drop-down menu on the Advanced toolbar and choose from the following options:

Changing the folder display

- Icons: displays each file as a separate picture (icon).
- Details: shows you the author, type and size of your file, plus the date it was last modified.
- By Author: sorts and groups files according to their author.
- By File Type: sorts and groups files according to what kind of files they are (Word documents, text files and so on).
- Document Timeline: slots your files into a calendar-style display, showing the date each file was last modified.
- Program: shows files which are self-contained programs or special system files only.

creating shortcuts on the Outlook Bar Create shortcuts to your frequently used folders by first right clicking the name of group you want to add the shortcut to (such as My Shortcuts). Choose Outlook Bar Shortcut from the menu and select the folder you want to create a shortcut to. Click OK.

With so many kinds of items in Outlook, it sometimes becomes hard to keep track of where your files are. Outlook allows you to perform complex and specific searches for items not only in Outlook but over your entire hard drive or network.

Performing a simple search

In the folder list or the Outlook Bar, click on the folder you would like to search in. For example, if you are looking for a mail message, click Inbox.

1 **Click** on the Tools menu and **select** Find.
2 In the Look for panel, **type** any text you want to search for in the fields listed on the left-hand side. To search through the actual content of items, **tick** the Search all text in the message checkbox.
3 **Click** Find Now.

To close the Find window, **click** on the x in the top right corner of the Find window.

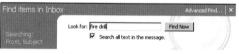

The Close button

Performing a simple search

Performing an advanced search

The Advanced Find facility allows you to narrow down your search and specify more than simply keywords you are looking for. To open an Advanced Find:

1 **Click** on the Tools menu.
2 **Select** Advanced Find.
3 In the Look for panel, **select** the type of item you are looking for (messages, notes, files and so on).
4 If you are searching for a file on your hard drive or network, **click** Browse and **select** a drive or folder to search in.

Using Advanced Find to search for a document on your hard drive

5 The panels below will change depending on what type of file you are looking for. **Type** in the keywords and any other information you are searching for.
6 **Click** on the More Choices and Advanced tabs for further search options.
7 When all your options are set, **click** on Find Now.

wild card searches If you only have partial information about a keyword or the name of a file, use the asterisk (*) as a 'wild card'. For example, if you want to search for keywords like market, marketing and markets, type market* in the Search for the word(s) panel and the search will find all variations of the word endings. Or, if you know you are looking for a Word document file but don't know its name, you can type *.doc in the Named panel.

I can't see my full Calendar entry

When you're using Outlook's Calendar, it may seem as if long entries have been truncated to fit the narrow column widths. However, if you hover your mouse over an entry you'll see full details of each entry appear, and when you print the Calendar, long entries will appear in full.

I can't see my Outlook Bar or List of folders

Both of these functions can be turned on or off whenever you like. **Click** on the View menu and **click** on either Outlook Bar or Folder List to view these features.

Outlook Today is coming up blank

One possible reason for the absence of Outlook Today in the view area is that you have cleared the option which displays this page. To fix this:
1 **Click** on the View menu and **click** Folder List if you can't already see it.
2 In the folder list, **right click** the Outlook Today folder and then **click** Properties.
3 In the Mailbox Properties dialog box, **click** the Home Page tab.
4 **Click** to select Show home page by default for this folder and then **click** OK.

My Journal has no entries in it

If you have been working on Office files and sending emails but still nothing appears in your Journal:
1 **Click** on the Tools menu and **choose** Options.
2 **Click** on Journal Options.
3 In the top left list, **select** which kind of items you would like to record and which contacts you would like them to apply to.
4 **Select** other file types from the bottom left list to include in your Journal.
5 **Click** OK.

I haven't received any responses to my meeting request

If you know people have responded to your request but you haven't received any emails, you may have an option selected which deletes meeting responses. To check this:
1 **Click** on the Tools menu and **choose** Options.
2 **Click** on the E-mail tab.
3 **Uncheck** the Delete receipts and blank responses after processing checkbox.
4 **Click** OK.

My personal folder files will not import or export

Error message: Properties for This Information Service Must Be Defined Prior to Use or File access is denied. You do not have permission required to access the file.

This is an error you may receive when trying to import or export a personal folder in Outlook. Its most likely cause is that your personal folder file (.pst) file has been marked as a Read Only file, meaning it cannot be edited or changed. To fix this:

1 **Click** on the Start menu, **move** your mouse up to Find and **click** on Files or Folders.
2 In the Look in box, **choose** your computer's hard drive (usually the C drive).
3 In the Named box, **type** *.pst and **click** on Find Now. You will now see a list of files with the .pst file extension.
4 **Right click** on the name of the file you had problems opening and **choose** Properties.
5 **Uncheck** the Read Only box.

If you could not see your .pst file in this list, it might mean that your folders are stored on your company's email server. In this case, contact your IT expert.

The recipients of my emails do not see formatting in my messages

If a recipient sees only an unformatted version of a formatted message you sent, or sees an unformatted version with an attachment that repeats the message text, it usually means that the recipient's email program doesn't support HTML. You can choose to send messages to these contacts in plain text only. To do this:

1 **Open** the contact's details (see page 17).
2 **Check** the Send using plain text box.

The pictures I send in my emails can't be seen by the recipients

If you insert a shortcut to an image rather than a copy of an image in an email, the recipients will not see the image. The best way to send a picture in an email is to insert it as an attachment. See page 14 for details. Also be aware that sometimes pictures produced on a Macintosh may not be able to be accessed by a PC, and vice versa. Files often need to be named with file extensions (for example, .jpg or .gif at the end of the file name) to be read by a PC. Macintosh computers do not require file extensions.

viruses and email attachments As the most popular email program around, Outlook is a main target for attacks from viruses. There's a simple way to protect yourself against virus infection: be very careful about opening any email attachments. You should save all attachments to your hard drive and scan them with an updated anti-virus program before opening them. To save an email attachment, click on the message in your Inbox, click on the File menu and choose Save Attachments.

attachment An external file such as a word processing document, spreadsheet or graphic image that is included with an email message. The attachment is extracted by the recipient. A normal text message can accompany the attached file.

browser A software program used to display documents on the Internet.

cc Abbreviation of Carbon Copy. Additional addresses that identical copies of your message will be delivered to.

click and drag To click the left mouse button and hold it down while you move the mouse pointer across the screen.

click or left click To click once on the left button on your mouse.

contact A person whose details you have saved in Outlook.

database A collection of data that is logically arranged by its contents into fields.

desktop The screen with icons and a blank area that you see when you turn on your computer.

dialog box A small screen that pops up to offer you options or information about the task you are doing.

double-click To click the left mouse button twice in rapid succession.

drop-down menu A menu that 'drops down' a list of options when you click on a small downward-facing arrow.

email A system that lets you create a message on a computer and send it to other computer users on a large, shared computer or network of computers.

encryption Using a mathematical code to scramble a message. Encryption is the best way of ensuring privacy for web-based transactions.

FAQ Stands for Frequently Asked Questions. Lists of common questions that have been asked.

host A computer on the Internet that is capable of sending and receiving data.

icon A small picture which can be clicked on to control programs and functions.

internet A global computer network connecting thousands of networks and millions of computers.

intranet A special network within an office (or worldwide) that only offers access only to members of that intranet. Often set up like a mini-Internet.

journal In Outlook, the Journal is a way of tracking your daily activities, including files you have worked on and emails you have sent.

LAN Acronym for Local Area Network; a small network of at least two computers, usually in the same location, and usually connected by cabling.

log on/in To sign onto a computer after establishing a connection via modem or other means. Most software programs store user name and password information so that logging in is automatic.

log out/off To terminate a connection to a computer.

macro A mini-program designed as a shortcut to a common task.

menu A list of options from which a user can choose an action.

modem An electronic device that translates information from computer data signals to signals that can be transported over telephone lines (and vice versa).

network A group of computers linked together to share information, software and hardware.

note In Outlook, a note is an electronic version of a 'sticky' note in which you can type reminders for yourself.

POP mail A method of accessing email using a client to retrieve mail from a server.

program One single piece of software devoted to one task or sets of tasks.

right click To click once on the right button of your mouse.

server Any computer on the Internet that provides a service to other computers.

SMTP The standard email protocol used on the Internet that transfers email from one host to another.

task In Outlook, a task is an activity that you or someone else must complete. Tasks can be used for your own work or can be assigned to others.

taskbar The bar across the bottom of your screen which begins with the Start menu icon and displays the programs you have open.

toolbar A bar across the top of an application window containing icons for various functions specific to that application. Many toolbars can be customised to suit your preferences.

virus A program designed as a prank or sabotage which runs on your computer without your permission and which usually damages your files.